Visual World

العالم المصور

I0172218

كُنْ مَعَ اللّه

Be with Allah

100+ Captivating Colouring Activities

for Finding Peace
in Prayer & Duʿā
and Strengthening
your Bond
with Allah

Mosaic Tree Press

ISBN 978-1-916524-63-7

All artwork was designed and licensed by Freepik.com

First printing, 2023

Published by Mosaic Tree Press
Browse our complete catalogue of publications at MosaicTree.org

Published by
Mosaic Tree Press

بسم الله الرحمن الرحيم

In the name of God, the Most Gracious, the Most Merciful

Contents

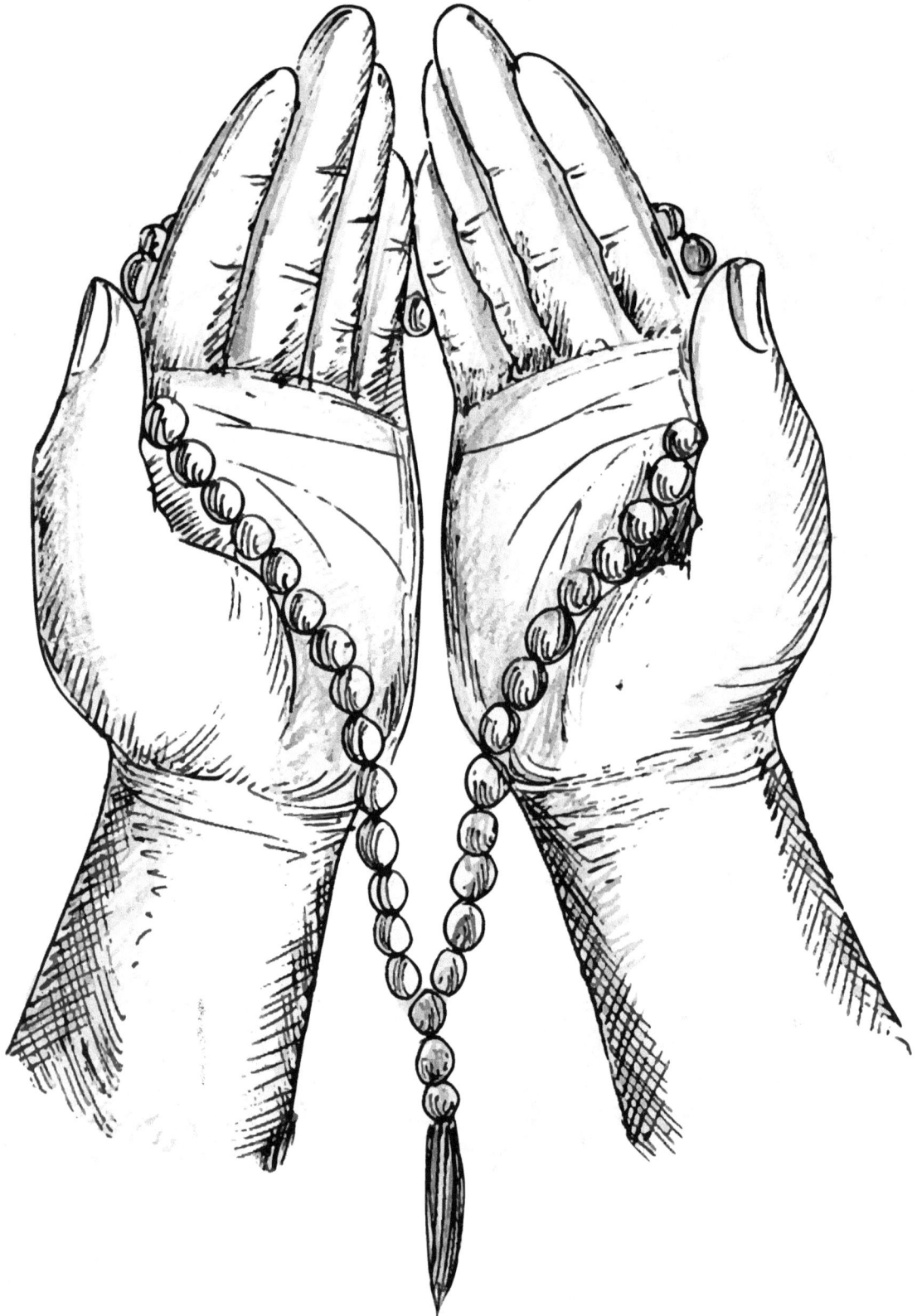

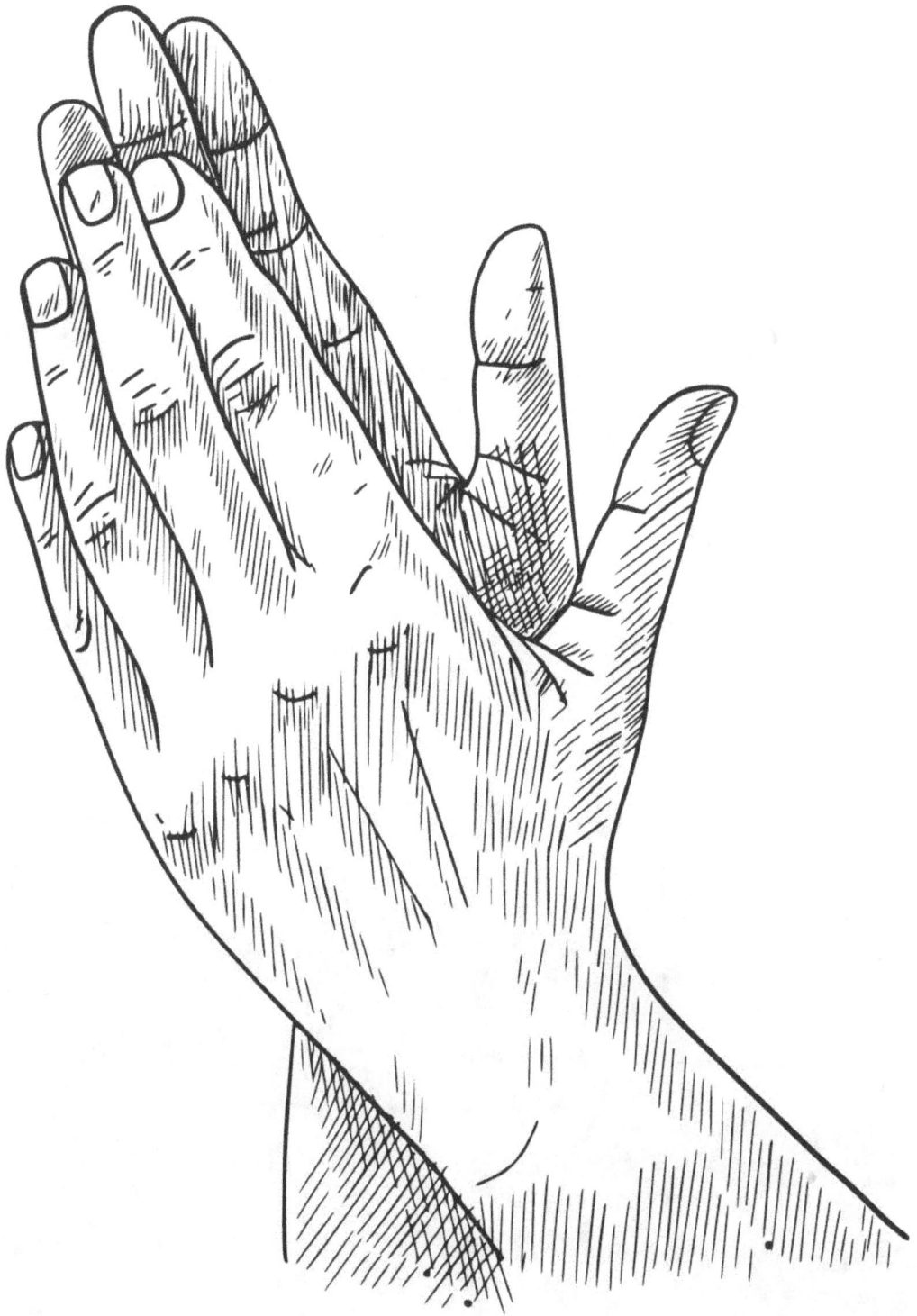

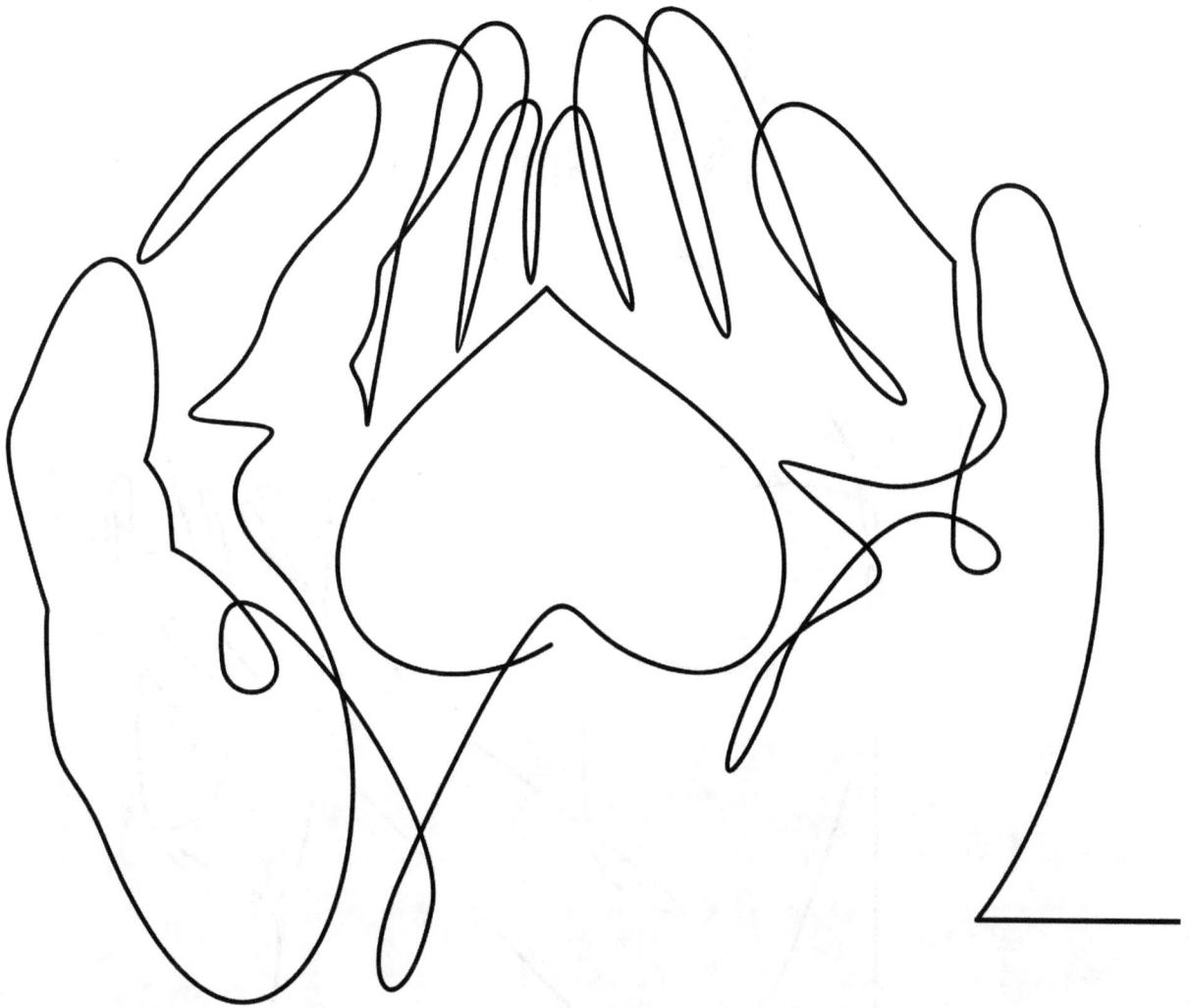

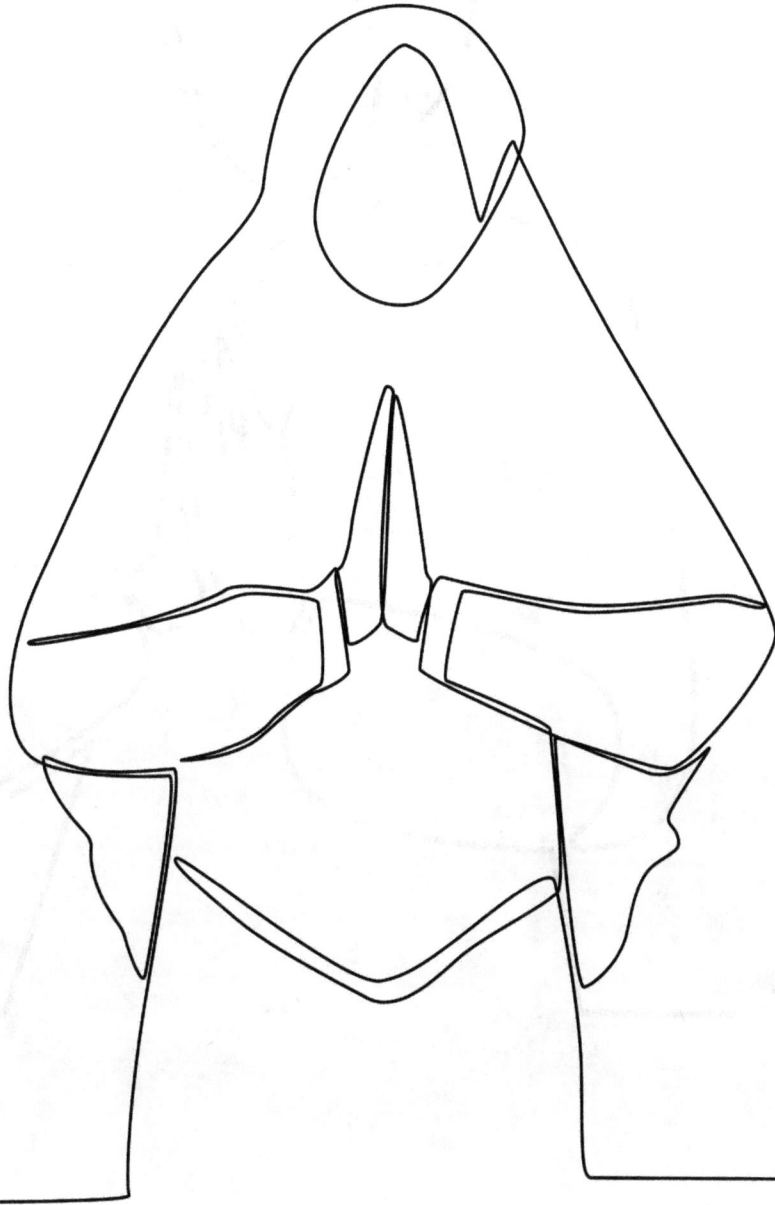

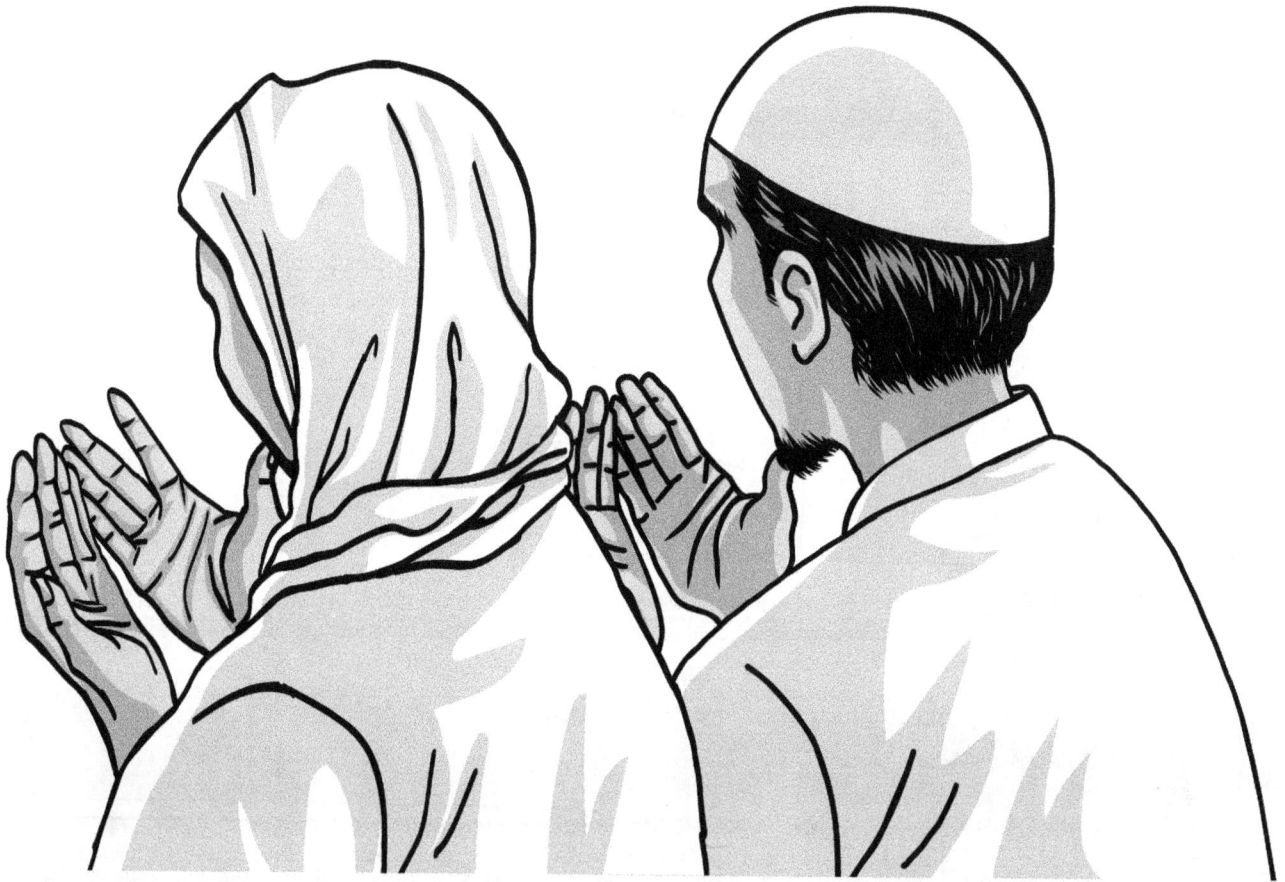

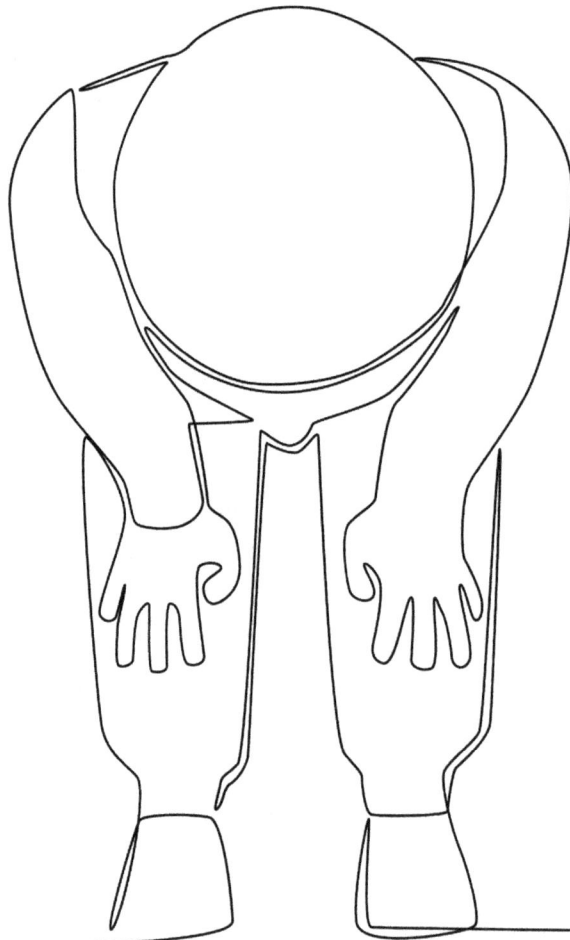

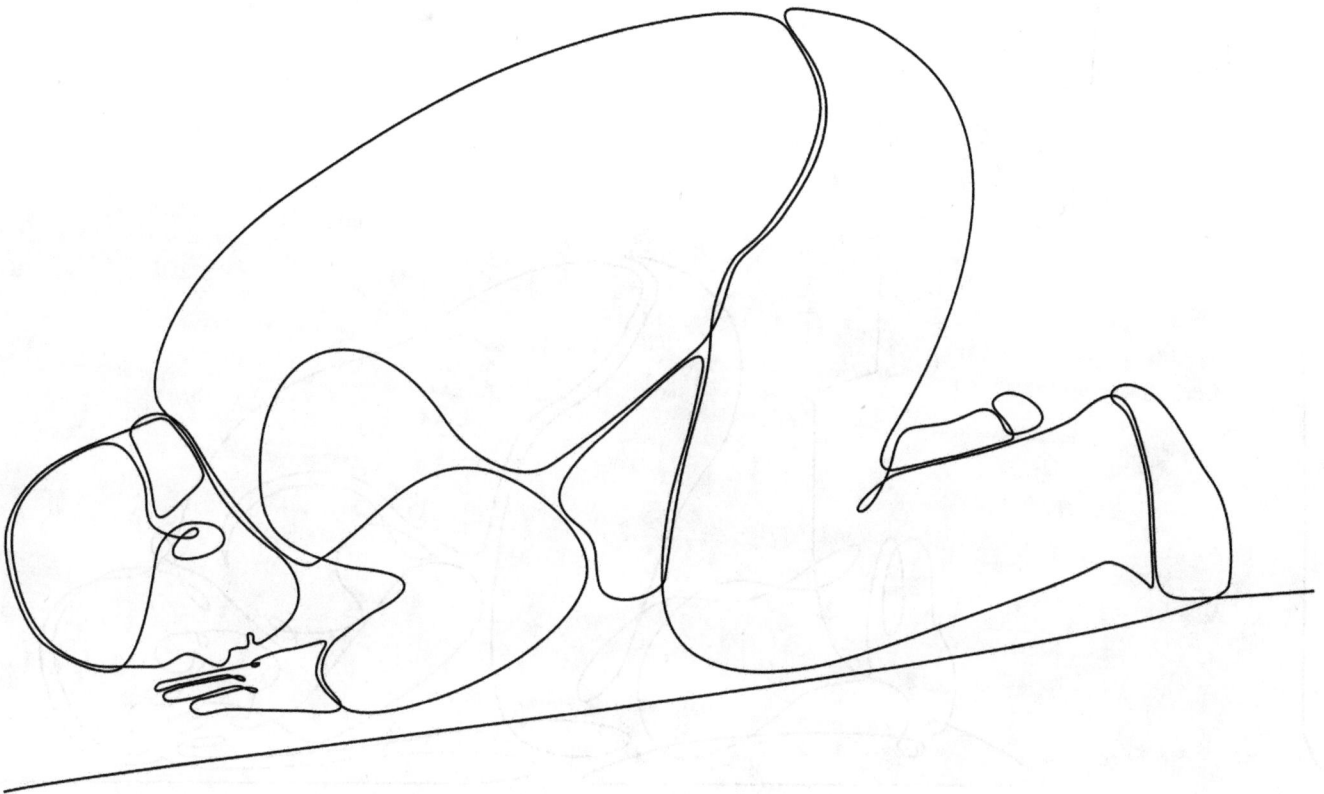

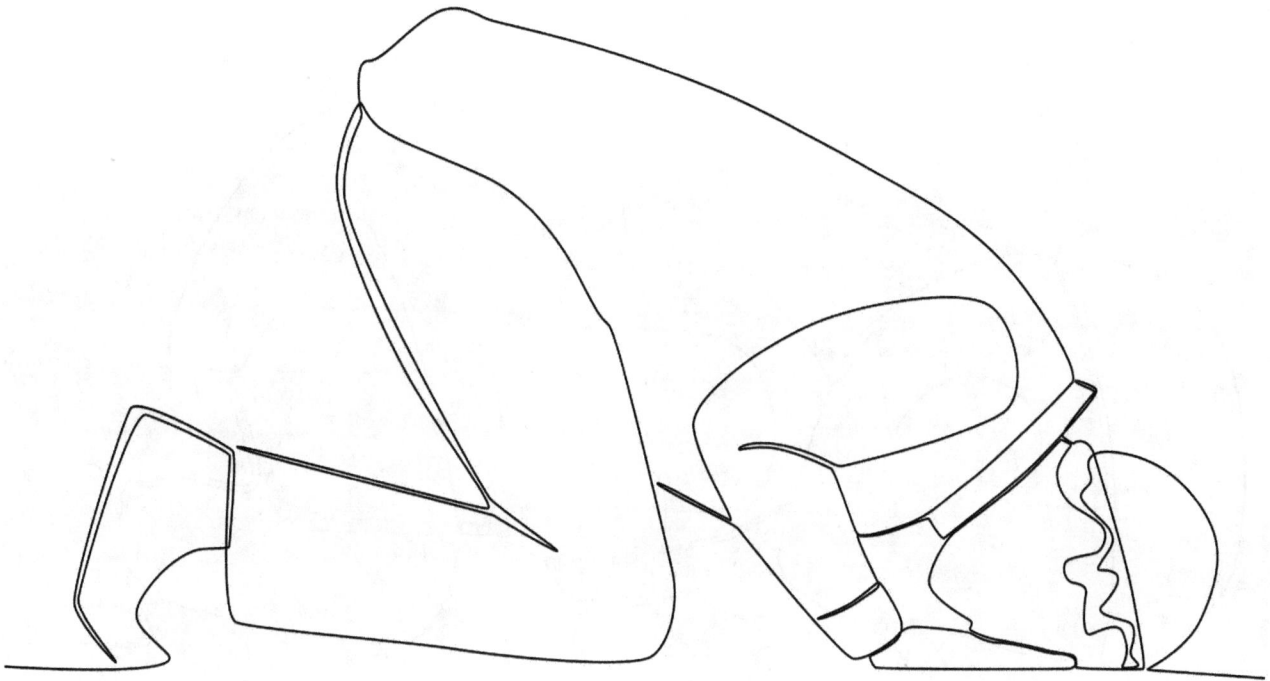

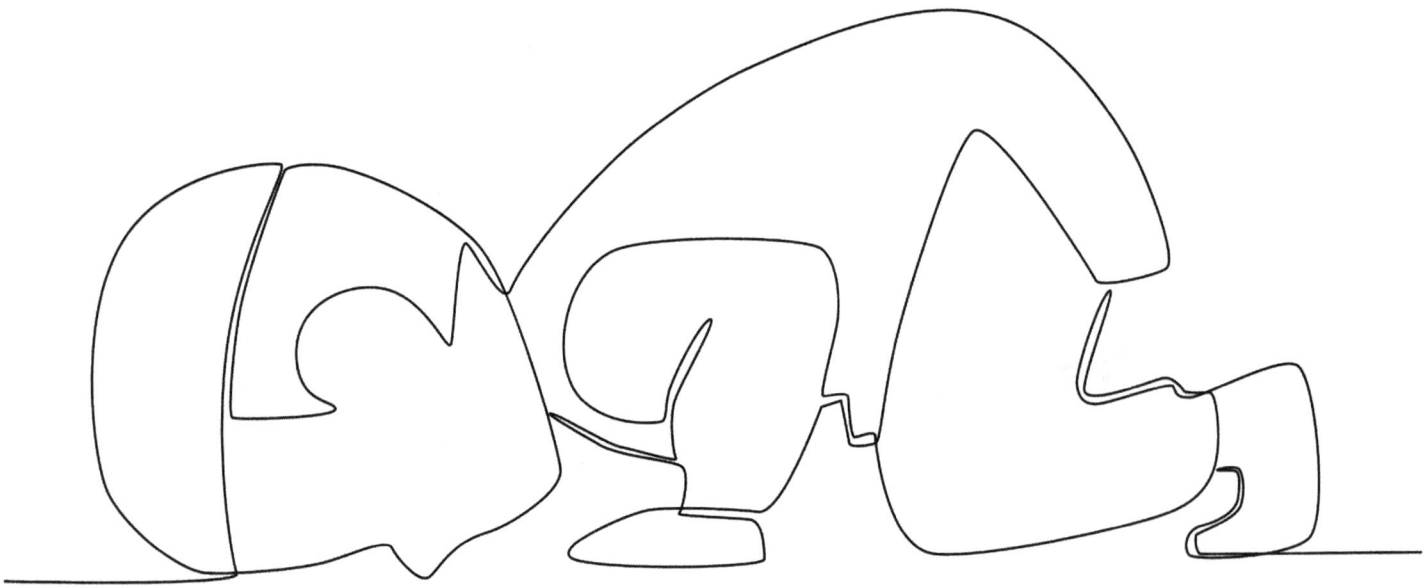

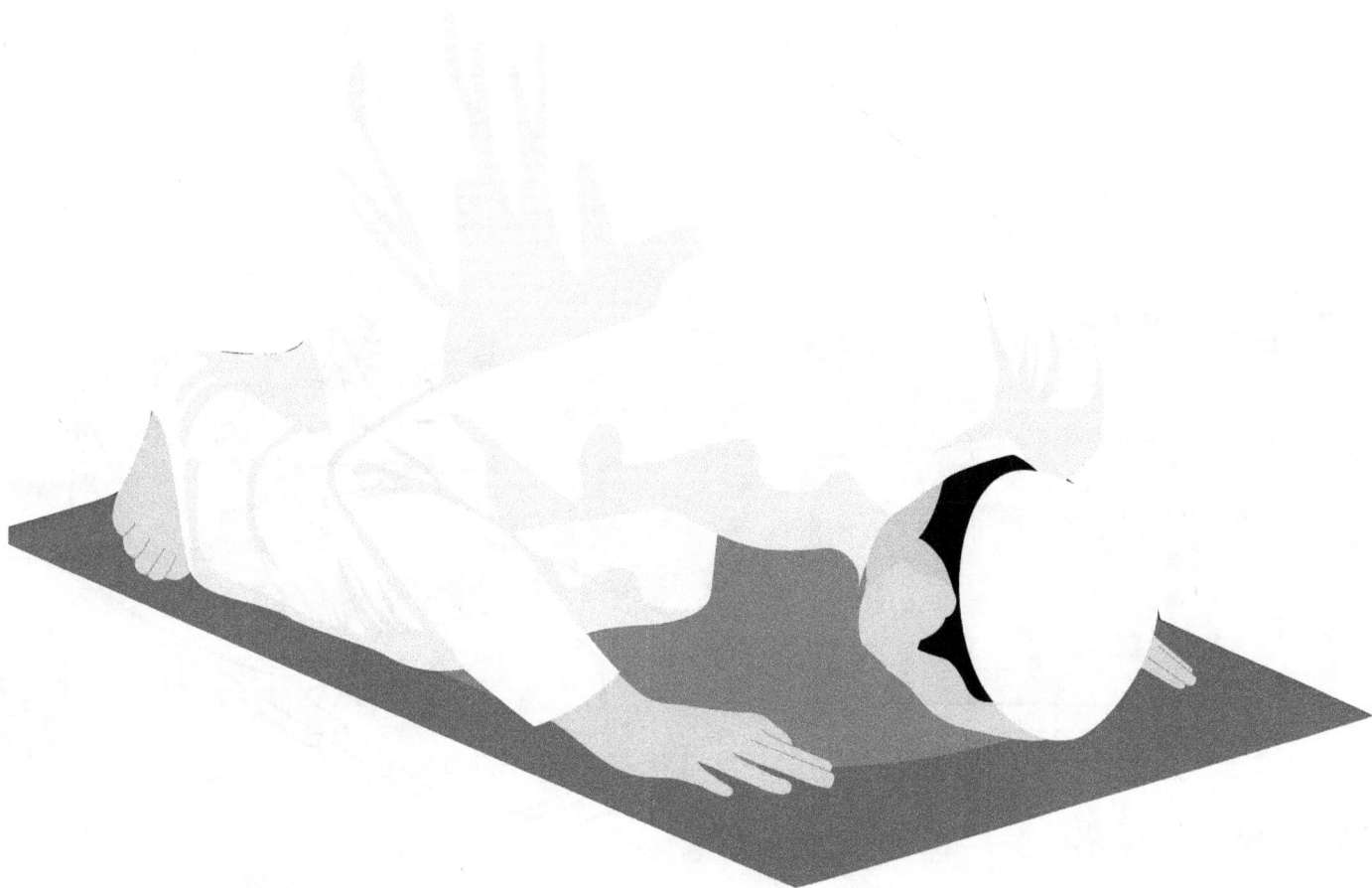

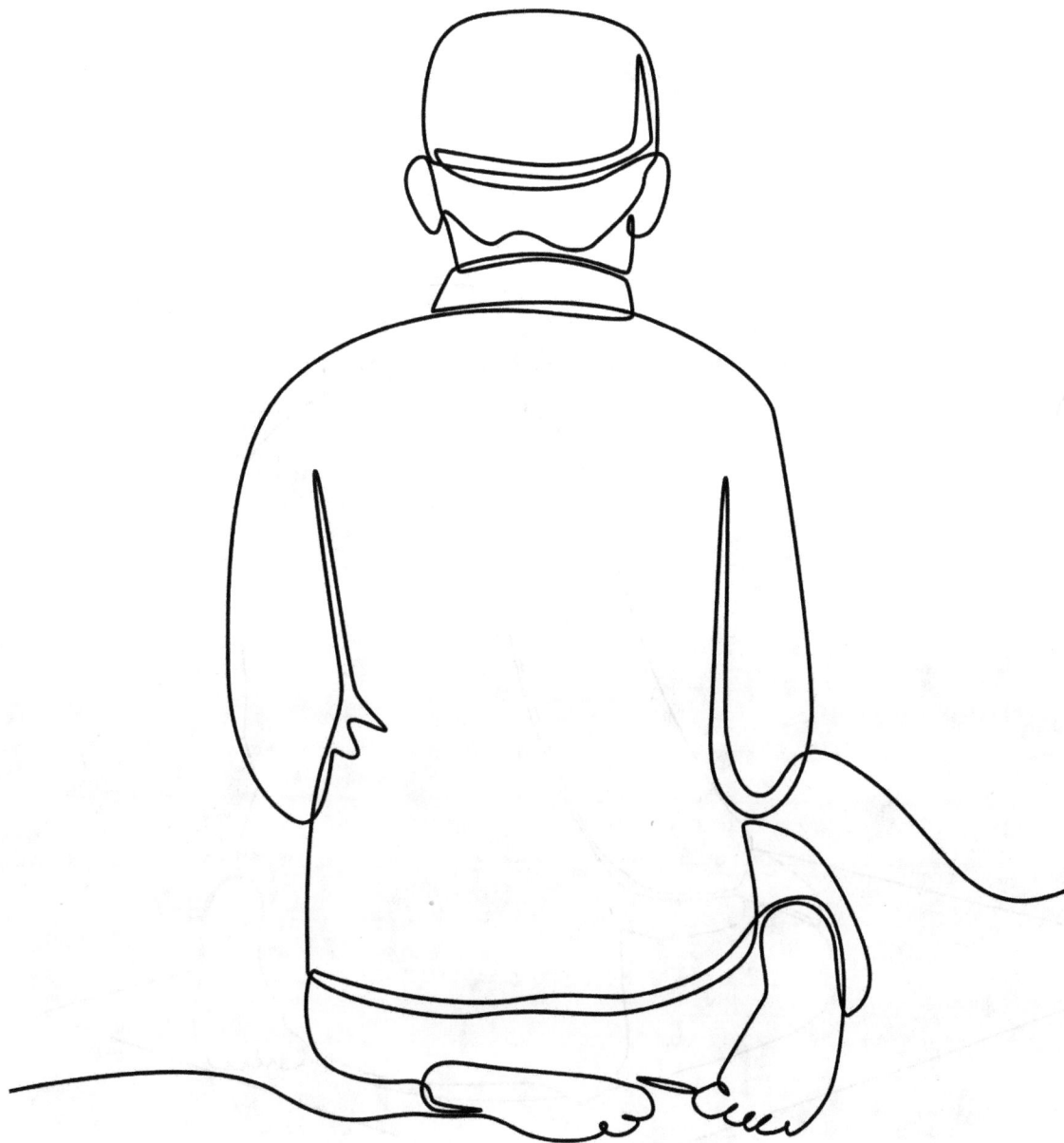

Eid
MUBARAK

Eid Mubarak

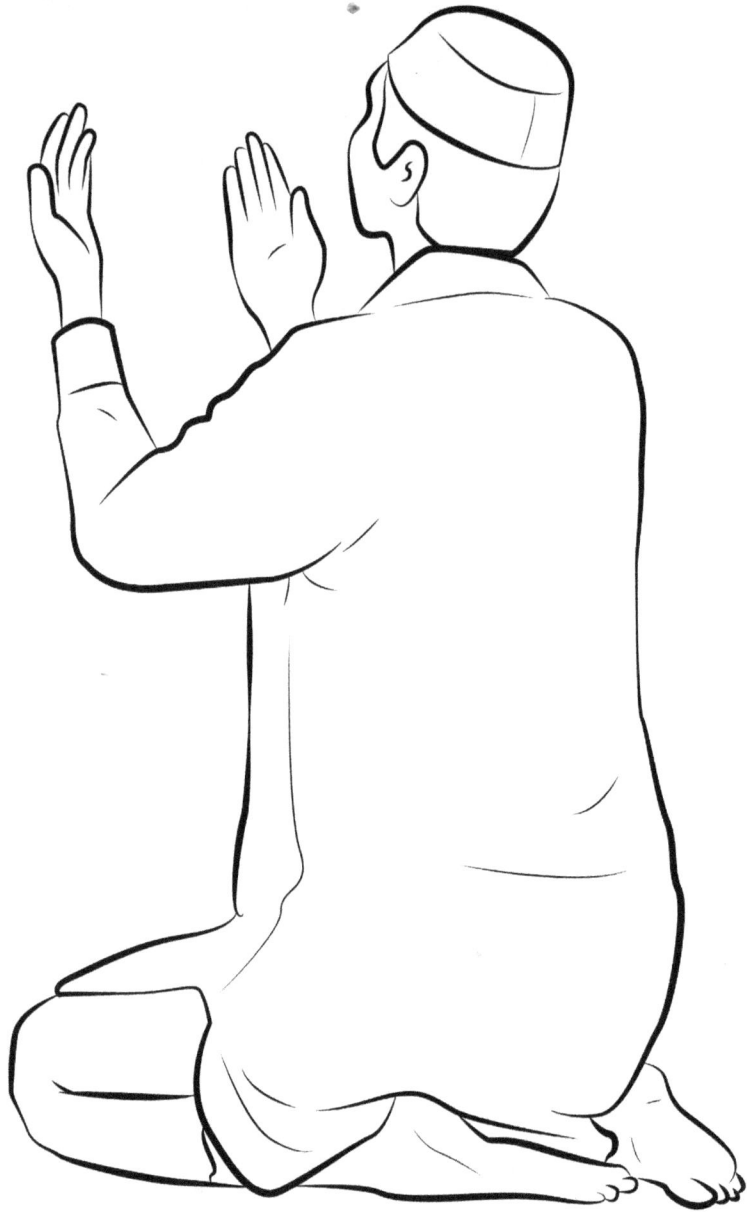

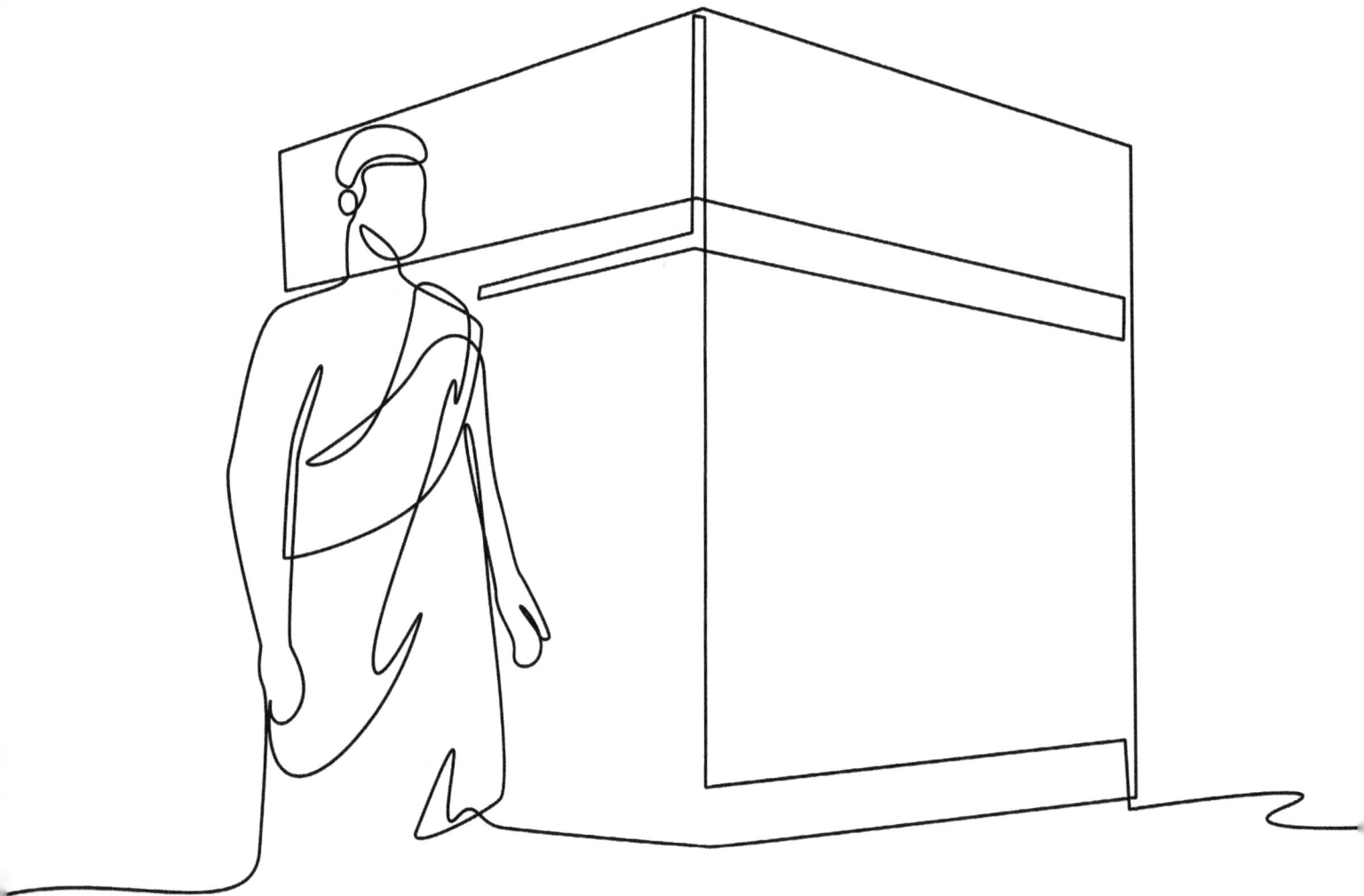

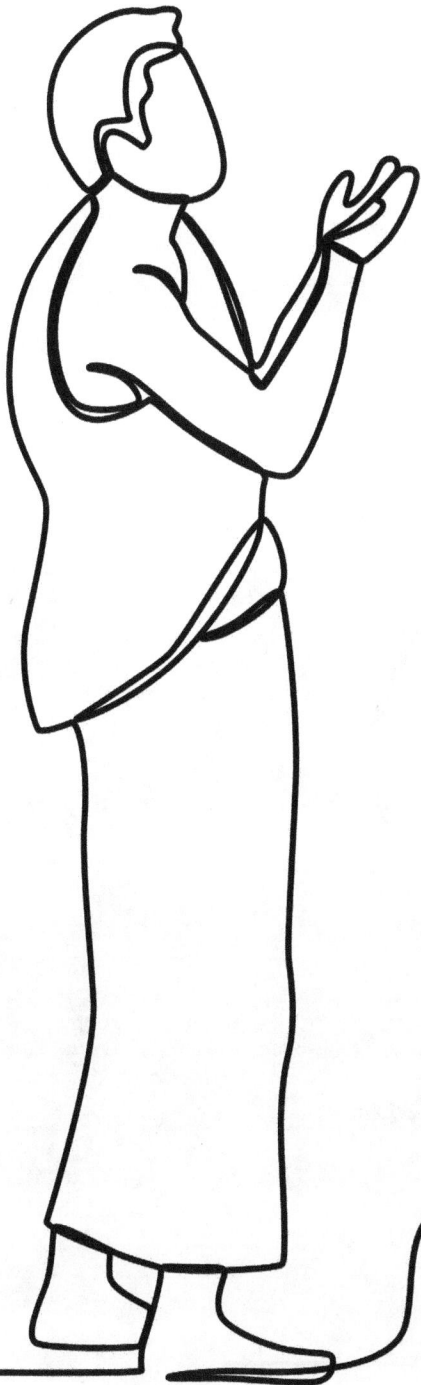

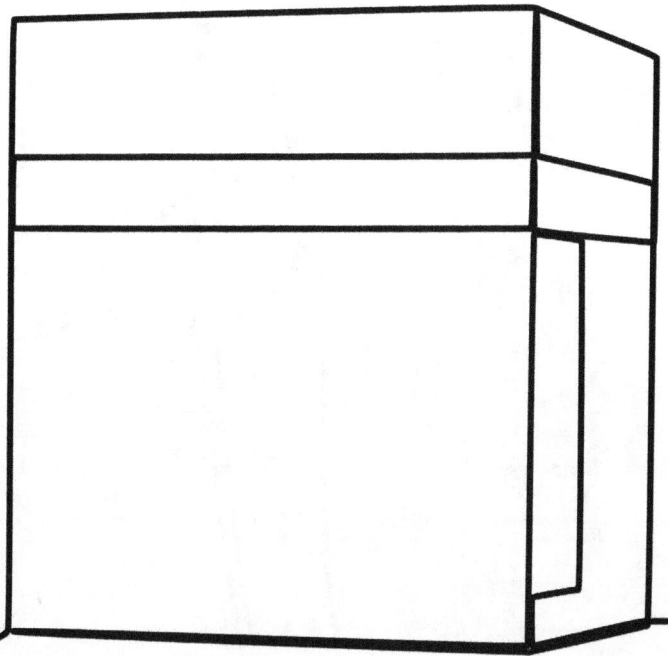

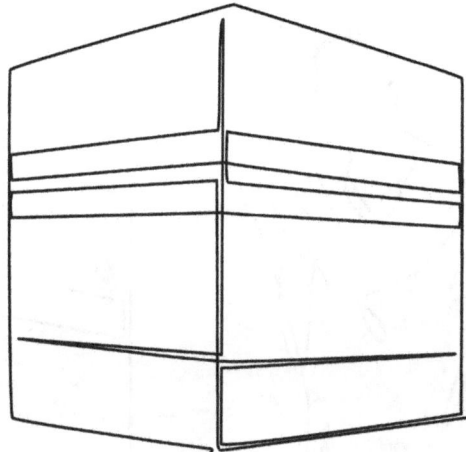

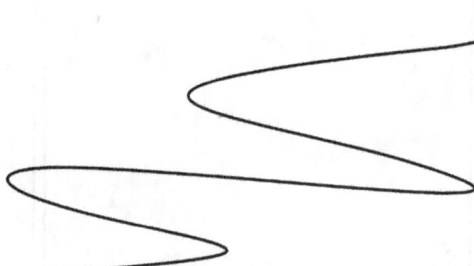

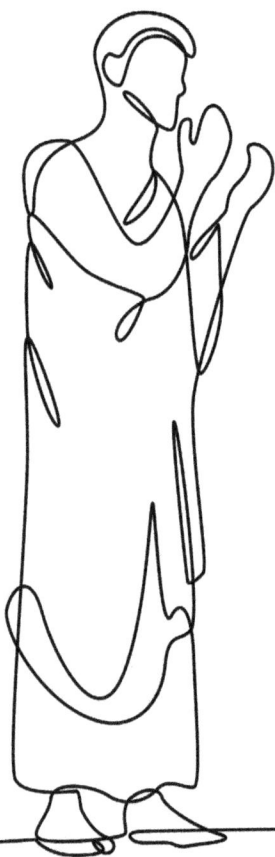

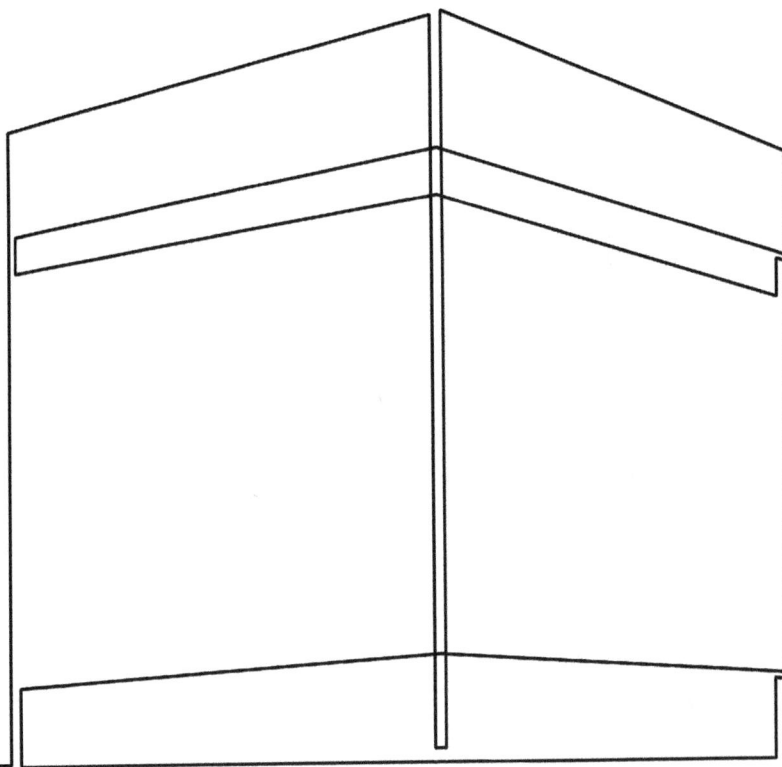

An ABC of Quotes About Palestine: Exploring Voices on Palestine & the Palestinian Quest for Justice (2023)

My First Arabic Numbers Reader & Colouring Book, Mosaic Tree Press (2023)

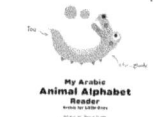

An Abc of Palestine: A Journey To Discover Palestine & The Palestinian People For Kids & Grown Ups (2023)

My First Arabic Colours: Reader & Activity Book for Kids, Mosaic Tree Press (2023)

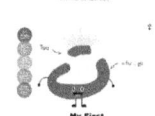

Palestine: 200+ Cut-Out & Collage Images for Arts & Crafts Activities (2023)

My Arabic Animal Alphabet Reader, Arabic for Little Ones, Mosaic Tree Press (2023)

Palestine: 50+ Colouring Activities to Celebrate Palestine & the Palestinian People (2023)

My First Arabic Alphabet Reader [Arabic for Little Ones] (2023)

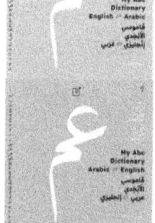

My Journey Through The Most Beautiful Names of Allah: Arabic Reader & Activity Book for Kids: **Volume 1, 2 & 3** (2023)

My Arabic Learning Journals: My Abc Dictionary (English-Arabic), Mosaic Tree Press (2022)

My First Arabic Alphabet & Colouring Book [Arabic for Little Ones] (2023)

My Arabic Learning Journals: My Abc Dictionary (Arabic- English), Mosaic Tree Press (2022)

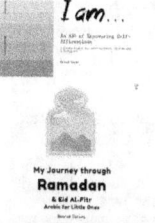

My First Arabic Alphabet: Letter Tracing & Colouring Book [Arabic for Little Ones] (2023)

My Arabic Learning Journals: Thematic Vocabulary, Mosaic Tree Press (2022)

Essential Arabic Readers: Alphabet Letters with Vowels & Pronunciation Symbols, Mosaic Tree Press (2022)

I Am .... An ABC of Empowering Self-Affirmations: A Guided Journal for Self-Discovery, Self-Growth & Resilience (2022)

Similar Sounding Letters in Arabic: Essential Arabic Readers (2023)

My Journey through Ramadan & Eid Al-Fitr (Arabic for Little Ones), Mosaic Tree Press (2023)

Essential Arabic Readers: Arabic Alphabet Writing Practice Handbook, Mosaic Tree Press (2023)

CoronaVirus Lexicon: A Practical Guide for Arabic Learners & Translators (M. Diouri & M. Aboelezz 2023)

Listen, Read & Write: Arabic Alphabet Letter Groups [Essential Arabic Readers] (2023)

Arabic & Islamic Mosaic & Calligraphy Colouring Journal (Volume 1: Islamic Quotes) (2022)

Browse our full catalogue at

MosaicTree.org

A / ع Arabic Script & Sounds

A-Z Arabic Vocabulary

Arabic for Little Ones

Arabic/Islamic Mosaic & Calligraphy

Arabic Learning Journals

Well-Being & Character Development

Mosaic Tree Press

MosaicTree.org

بحمد الله تم

Completed with the grace of God

www.ingramcontent.com/pod-product-compliance
Lightning Source LLC
Chambersburg PA
CBHW081642040426

42449CB00015B/3419